# Dad's War

G000070719

# A schoolboy's diaries of the Second World War
# Volume I

## John Pritchard-Jones

prepared for publication by his daughter

Siân Pritchard-Jones

# Dad's War

# A schoolboy's diaries of the Second World War
# Volume I

## John Pritchard-Jones

prepared for publication by his daughter

Siân Pritchard-Jones

First edition: 04 August 2021; ISBN: 9798539652722

Published by Expedition World; www.expeditionworld.com; sianpj@hotmail.com

**Front cover photo:**   War planes from the Second World War
**Back cover photos:**   Safety instructions on the back of the 1939 exercise book
Some ancient tweets
**Above photo:**   John and Siân, aged 5¾ months exactly!

BRITAIN DECLARED WAR ON GERMANY at
11 a.m. on SUNDAY, SEPT. 3rd 1939.

# Diary of the War

## September 4, 1939

Two air-raid warnings. Athenia was torpedoed and shelled without warning by German submarine. On the same morning came news of the first two actions by the R.A.F. At the entrance to the Kiel Canal, two German warships have been bombed. Direct hits with heavy bombs are claimed. Some failed to return. British planes over Western and Northern Germany dropped more than 6,000,000 copies of a note to the German people. They came back unchallenged.

German airforce continues heavy bombing of Polish towns. London's evacuation is complete.

<u>September 5, 1939.</u>

The first fighting on the Western front. French prepare for an attack on Germany's Siegfried Line. 30 Polish planes bombed Berlin and returned safely. Germans advancing in the corridor and Silesia. Their mechanised troops have reached a point 56 miles from Warsaw. At Westerplatte, the small Polish troops hold out for the fifth day against 10,000 Germans. Paris has its first air-raid alarm. In U.S.A. the arms embargo prohibits the export of planes. South Africa joins in with Britain. The British steamer Bosnia (2,400 tons) is sunk without warning by an U-boat

<u>September 6, 1939.</u>

French advance begins. French are fighting on German soil.

Allied aircraft heavily bomb Rhineland
and Saar towns. Warsaw is in danger.
R.A.F. made leaflet raid on German territory
September 7, 1939

Cracow has fallen to the
Germans. Westerplatte surrenders. South
Africa declares war on Germany. French
advance continues
September 8, 1939

Cinemas are to re-open
Warsaw prepares for a siege. 150,000
German troops transferred from Poland
to the Western Front. French advance. R.A.F.
make another leaflet raid on German territory
3 British and 1 French merchant ships
sunk by submarine. Russia
mobilising on her Western frontier.
September 9, 1939

Britain prepares for a
3-year War. German mechanised

troops have reached the suburbs of Warsaw.
French occupie Forest of Warndt in
the Saar, and advance 8 miles
September 10, 1939

German attack checked.
in Poland. French troops launch attacks
between the Saar and Vosges. 15 large
towns and industrial areas have fallen
to the Germans. They are at the gates of
Warsaw. The Polish armies are retiring
to the Marshlands of the East. French
advancing. In 1 week the French have
occupied 350 square miles of German
territory

The Second Week        Sept. 11th 1939

British troops arrived in France. Warsaw
holds out. Four more British cargo steamers
have been sunk by enemy submarines.
Germans bombing all open towns in Poland

**The Man Who will Lead Our Armies in the Field**
General Viscount Gort, V.C. (right) leaving th[e]
Office. He was appointed Commander-in-C[hief]
British Field Forces the day war [...]

Air battles take place. Russian troop concentration on Polish Frontier. Number of German submarines sunk. French attacking Saarbrucken. Russia invades Poland. Polish troops pushed back. H.M.S. Courageous sunk by U-boat. Our oldest aircraft-carrier. (22,500 tons)

**The Polish Leader**
Major Koscianski, commander of the heroic garrison, passes on the orders of German officers

5

She carried 48 aircraft. Warsaw is nearly surrounded.

---

## Third Week.                    Sept. 16th. 1939

Germans and ~~British~~ Russian troops meet at Brest-Litovsk. Later Germans withdraw leaving Brest-Litovsk in the hands of the Soviet. Poland is breaking up. Hitler speaks at Danzig. Polish resistance collapsing everywhere except Warsaw. Russians take all of the Rumanian border cutting off German oil supplies. Germans bomb Warsaw ~~insee~~ incessantly. Rising has started in Bohemia, Moravia, and Western Slovakia. The Czechs did great damage to factories, machinery, buildings, roads, bridges, and railways. President Roosevelt ends arms embargo. Calinescu, Rumanian Premier is ~~asso~~ assinated by members of the Iron Guard. A Soviet-Nazi agreement is

**On the Outskirts of Warsaw**

No easy prey was the straggling city of Warsaw, whose population fight with greater ferocity as their chance of rescue fades. In spite of flame-throwers and tanks, German units are repulsed time and again.

signed on their zones in Poland. The Suprem War-Council met. The demarcation line follows the rivers Piasa, Narew, Vistula, and San.

Russia gets the lust part. Gen. Baron von Fitsch, a former commander-in-chief of the German army is killed. Warsaw holds out. Petrol rationing begins in Britain. Great criticism of the government.

<u>Fourth Week</u>　　　　　<u>Sept. 25th 1939</u>

The battle of Warsaw is nearly ending. The city is in flames. French begin a

heavy bombardment of German
fortifications along the Rhine.
Air battles
continue
to take place.
French war-
planes bomb
Friedrichshaven
R.A.F make
another
leaflet raid.
We have
siezed 67,000

The Path of the Invader
Bridges at the front are destroyed by the retreating Polish armies.
Bridges behind the lines are blown up by German bombers to cripple
transport of reinforcements.

tons of German merchandise more than we
have lost. Sir John Simon issues his first
war budget. Many thousands of Polish
refugees cross the Roumanian frontier.
Warsaw falls to the Germans after 22
days of merciless siege. An agreement
is signed between. Estonia accepts Soviet

protection, and places naval base s at their disposal. R.A.F raids the German at Heligoland. 3 more neutral ships are sunk by U-boat. New Polish President. General Sikorski to be Premier and Commander of the Polish Army in France. All Polish resistance has broken down.

A Field Gun Inside a German Pillbox

Some pillboxes in the Siegfried line are large enough to hold a field gun. Only by tremendous concentration of artillery fire can they be broken down.

Fifth Week        Oct. 2nd 1939

Russia demands bases for Finland.
British freighter sunk by an armed
German raider off Brazil. French
capture the Forest of Borg. Hitler
makes peace speech. No success.

Sixth Week        Oct. 9th 1939

Finland evacuates her main cities.
Battle between British fleet and Germans
bombers in the North Sea. 3 U-boats
sunk in one day.
H.M.S. Royal Oak
(29,000 tons) battleship
was sunk by
torpedoes. The French
steamers, Loisiane, and
Bretagne. and the
British steamer
Lochavon have been

The War Premier Who Pleads For Peace
Mr. Lloyd George with his ploughman at his
farm at Churt.

10

sink by U-boat.

## Seventh Week     Oct 16th 1939

German bombing planes reach Britain
Bomb Firth of Forth, Scapa Flow and the
Orkneys. Germans launch an attack
Food prices rise. Pact with Turkey is
signed. Air battle over North Sea. 5 Nazi
planes brought down during the week.

## Eighth Week.     Oct 23rd 1939

Soviet-Finnish negotiations
resumed. Von Ribbentrop speaks at
Danzig. U.S. merchant ship, City of
Flint, is seized by German destroyer.
Taken to Murmansk. Two German
pocket-battleships, Deutschland and
Graf Spee are loose in the Atlantic.
troops are German troops massing on
frontiers of Holland, Belgium and Switzerland

German plane shot down over the
Firth of Forth. The first British wounded
come home.

## Ninth Week    Oct. 30th 1939

British destroyers beat off German
bombers. Finland has rejected the
Russian proposals. The U.S.A. arms embargo is lifted. Soviet warn Finland. The U.S.A merchant - man City of Flint

On the Western Front
Camouflaging French artillery in the battle-zone.    Over the net will be
spread leaves and branches to hide them from enemy planes.

is seized by a German raider in the

Atlantic. She was taken to Murmansk, by a Nazi prize crew. ~~Sailer~~ She was caught in Norwegian waters, and the German prize crew were interned. She was set free.

## Tenth Week          Nov. 6th 1939

French fighters shoot down 9 German fighters. Holland and Belgium fear invasion by Germany. Fifteen minutes after Hitler left Munich beerhall a bomb explodes. Nazi planes drop pamphlets over ~~France~~. Holland floods main defences. The first war-time Armistice Day. Mr. Churchill speaks on the war.

## Eleventh Week.          Nov. 13th 1939

~~First~~ bombs are dropped on British soil, during two raids on the Shetlands.

13

Two German steamers are scuttled by their crews to avoid capture, and two others are captured. Two U-boats are sunk. Germans are laying mines. Britain loses a destroyer, a cargo-boat, and a steamer. Russians allege that the Finnish Government were preparing for war against Russia. Nazi raider sunk British tanker off East African coast. Revolt flares up in Czechoslovakia and Austria. The "Simon Bolivar" (8,309 ton) was sunk by a mine. 140 people lost their lives. Germans are using magnetic mine.

## Twelfth Week                    Nov. 20th 1939

German seaplanes drop magnetic mines off the East Coast. The Japanese liner Terukuni Maru (11,930 tons) is sunk by a mine. U-boat sinks British

minesweeper, and three Fleetwood trawlers.
H.M.S. Gipsy sunk by a mine. The
war costs £6 million a day. Allied air
forces shoot down 19 German planes.
British cruiser BELFAST damaged by
mine. The RAWALPINDI and the PILSUDSKI
are sunk. French Navy sunk 3 U-boats
and a German cargo-ship was
scuttled.

## Thirteenth Week.          Nov. 27th 1939

R.A.F. planes raid Borkum. Navy
captures two German ships. RUSSIA INVADES
FINLAND. Field-Marshal Mannerheim is
appointed Commander-in-Chief of the
Finnish Army. Many air-raids on Finnish
towns. Britain calls up 250,000 more
men, 22 years old. 3 more U-boats are
sunk and 1 captured.

## Fourteenth Week

The King goes to France. Britain sends 100 Spitfires to Finland, and Italy 50. R.A.F. drive off German bombers who were over the Firth of Forth estuary. Fighting in the Artic Circle.

## Fifteenth Week
NovDec 13th 1939

The League of Nations expel Russia. R.A.F. planes shoot down 17 German fighters. Our losses are 10. There is a battle between a German battleship and British cruisers in the South Atlantic. The German pocket-battleship GRAF SPEE was engaged by the cruisers, EXETER, AJAX, and ACHILLES. Late at night the GRAF SPEE was forced into Montevideo badly damaged. Finns kill 36,000 Russians in a battle. On December 17 the GRAF

SPEE steams out, and there is a violent
explosion on board and the GRAF SPEE is
scuttled on the personal orders of Hitler.
The British submarine SAMON sighted
the German liner BREMEN but did
not sink it, but it sunk a U-boat
and torpedoed the German cruiser LEIPZIG
and damaged a heavy cruiser. Another
submarine the URSULA sunk a German
cruiser. The German liner COLUMBUS
was scuttled by her crew. Two more U-boats
were sunk by the French destroyer SIROCCO.

<u>Sixteenth Week</u>     <u>Dec. 20<sup>th</sup> 1939</u>

Captain Langsdorf, ~~shoots to~~ Commander of
the GRAF SPEE shoots himself. The German heavy
cruiser BLUCHER has been damaged by
torpedo. Soviet offensive in Finland fails.
Two more serious railway crashes in
Germany. This is the 10<sup>th</sup> since the outbreak

17

of the war.

**And from the Russians, the Finns Capture Bread**
Finnish soldiers, wearing white cloaks to make them invisible against the snow, inspect loaves of bread taken from an overturned lorry. The lorry was abandoned by the Russian troops after an attack.

A great earthquake in Anatolia, Turkey. 20,000 are killed. The first Christmas of the war. British cargo-ship torpedoed. R.A.F attacks German warships. Sugar and meat will be rationed on January 8th. More Finnish successes. A British battleship is slightly damaged by torpedo. New classes to registered.

Seventeenth Week    Jan. 1st 1940
U.S.A. send Finland 400 planes. Mr. Hore-Belisha resigns. Mr. Oliver Stanley takes his place. Russians digging-in in the Karelian Isthmus It is the first day of rationing

Eighteenth Week  Jan 9th 1940
Commander is Air-Marshal A.S. Barratt is to be commander of the R.A.F. in France. Spain sends arms to Finland. R.A.F. bomb Sylt. Germans try to penetrate the Firth of Forth, but are

Mr. Oliver Stanley
The new War Minister in place of Mr. Hore-Belisha. He is 44, has held five Ministerial posts in nine years. He is little known to the public. He is a son of Lord Derby and son-in-law of the Marquess of Londonderry.

driven off. The British lines. DUNBAR CASTLE (10,000 tons) is sunk by a mine. R.A.F. planes have flown over Austria and Bohemia, and dropped leaflets on Vienna, and Prague. R.A.F. bomb German destroyers in Heligoland Bight. Tension over Holland and Belgium.

## Nineteenth Week     Jan. 15th 1940

Mass raids by Russian bombers have begun in Finland. There is a great frost all over Northern Europe. Allies order 8,000 planes from U.S.A. Rumania has built a 300 mile moat round her frontiers. There is an explosion in an Exeter Munitions Factory. Finnish armies claim more victories. Balkan manoevres. Mr. Churchill and Lord Halifax make speeches. The British destroyer, GRENVILLE is sunk by a mine or torpedo. Italy is to spend £436,000,000 on defence.

---

## Twentieth Week                    Jan. 22nd 1940

Germany obtains control of the former Polish territory on the Rumanian frontier from Russia. H.M. Destroyer EXMOUTH is sunk by a mine or torpedo. It is the fifth since the war began. Finns bomb Kronstadt. Sweden helps Finland.

. . . But Exercises Go On

Revolver practice in the snow for British troops in France. Nearly all the fighting so far has been between small patrols at night. And the revolver has proved more useful in this kind of fighting than the rifle.

Bacon ration to be doubled.

Twenty-first Week     Jan. 29. 1940
U-boat is sunk. The tanker
VACLITE (5,026 tons) is sunk. British
warplanes being sent to Finland. The Balkan Conference ends.

. . . And A Finished Product
Torpedo heads at a factory in England. Each torpedo has over 6,000 parts. These
heads carry the explosives which make the torpedo such a deadly weapon.

Twenty-second Week     Feb. 5. 1940
Allied war council meets. Rationing

of butcher's meat to begin on March 11th.
British volunteers will soon be fighting
in Finland. President Roosevelt is to send
Mr. Sumner Welles on a tour of Britain,
France, Germany and Italy. Two U-boats
sunk.

Twenty-third Week Feb 12th 1940
New Soviet —
German trade
pact. Australian
and New Zealand
Expeditionary
Force lands at
Suez. 2 U-boats
sunk. Russian
troops advance.
400 British
sailors are
rescued from a

The Genius of German Warplanes
Messerschmitt (right), designer of Germany's
best fighters, with Hess. He has invented a
faster warplane, say German reports.

the German ship ALTMARK. by the British destroyer COSSACK. They are the crews of merchant-ships which the GRAF SPEE sunk.

## Twenty-fourth Week     Feb. 19th 1940
The British destroyer DARING is torpedoed with the loss of 157 lives. British trawlers are armed against air attack. Russians still advancing. Russians around Viborg. Crews of AJAX and EXETER arrive home.

## The Twenty-fifth Week     Feb. 26th 1940
R.A.F. planes have flown over the German Baltic seaports for the first time. There is a great battle for Viborg. Rationing begins in France. Mr. Sumner Welles arrives in Berlin. The Indian steamer DOMALA (8,441 tons)

is bombed by a German plane
108 people are missing.

## The Twenty-sixth Week    March 4th 1940
Italian coal-ships are stopped.
The British liner QUEEN ELIZABETH arrived
safely on her maiden voyage from
Britain accross the Atlantic. Allies
order more U.S. planes. There are
rumors of a Russo-Finnish peace talks.
Mr. Sumner-Welles meets President
Lebrun and M. Daladier.

## The Twenty-seventh Week    March 9th 1940
Mr. Sumner Welles meets Mr. Chamberlain.
Russo-Finnish peace announced. The
terms are :-
1. Hostilities to cease at noon on Wednesday
2. Finland to cede the whole of the
Karelian Isthmus, including Viborg, and

the shores of Lake Ladoga.

  3. Finland to cede the Rybachi Peninsula in the far North, but to retain Petsamo.

  4. The Island of Hango to be leased to Russia for 30 years as a military and air base.

  5. To give Russia a direct railway link with the richest mineral areas in Sweden.

  6. The Soviet to confiscate important industrial undertakings in Finland.

  7. Treaty of non-aggression to be signed.

  8. ✗ Sir Michael O'Dwyer is shot dead by an Indian.

---

### The Twenty-eight Week    March 16ᵗʰ
Hitler and Mussolini meet at Brenner Pass. Germans raid Scapa Flow. One warship slightly damaged. R.A.F. bomb Sylt.

<u>The Twenty-ninth week</u>          <u>March 24th 1940</u>

France has a new Government headed by M. Reynaud.
Denmark loses 7 ships. Two German ore ships are
sunk. Mr. Sumner Welles returns to Washington.

<u>The Thirtieth Week.</u>          <u>March 31st 1940</u>

The New Air Minister Visits An R.A.F. Station
In the Cabinet re-shuffle, Sir Samuel Hoare gets his old job of Air Minister.

The Norwegian Parliament sits in secret session. There are many Cabinet changes. Big shipbuilding drive. German warships bombed at Wilhelmshaven 5 enemy machines are shot down over the Western Front.

# The Thirty-first Week
## April 8th 1940

### Mines are laid off the coast of Norway

**"Gneisenau," Sunk by Gun Fire**
26,000 ton sister-ship of the "Scharnhorst."
Sunk by Norwegians in Oslo Fjord.

**"Admiral Scheer," Torpedoed**
10,000 ton pocket-battleship, launched in
1933, sister-ship of "Graf Spee."

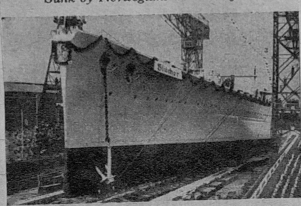

**"Blücher," Sunk by Mine**
10,000 ton cruiser "Blucher" hit by
Norwegian batteries. Later struck mine.

**"Karlsruhe" Sunk by Submarine**
6,000 ton cruiser, torpedoed by the
British submarine H.M.S. "Truant."

## GERMANY INVADES NORWAY AND DENMARK.

During the night, German warships force

"Scharnhorst" badly hammered
Caught by the battle cruiser "Renown,"
the 26,000 ton cruiser "Scharnhorst"
was heavily hit and put to flight.

their way up Oslo fiord.
Four ports, Narvik, Bergen,
Stavanger, Trondheim, are
captured by the Germans.
The Norwegian Parliament
decides to fight on. Oslo
falls. Two naval engage-
ments are reported off
Norway and the Skagerak.
The GNEI Two German cruisers
are sunk, a British destroyer and another ashore.
The GNEISENAU, a German battleship is sunk by
gunfire. Denmark surrenders with little fighting.
At Narvik there is a battle between British destroyer
and German warships. H.M.S. HUNTER is sunk. HARDY
and HOTSPUR slightly damaged. British navy has
occupied Faroe Islands and is guarding Iceland.
R.A.F. attack German warships in Christiansand Fiord.
Britain has laid a vast minefield to seal up the
Baltic Sea. The WARSPITE led the second destroyer

flotilla into Narvik Fiord and sunk 4 German destroyers. German soldiers escaping to the hills. ADMIRAL SCHEER attacked and the KARLSRUHE sunk.

<u>The Thirty-second Week</u>     <u>April 15<sup>th</sup> 1940</u>

British troops land in Norway. Stavanger bombed by the R.A.F. German ships bombed in Oslo Fiord. Allied reinforcements on the way. There is a great battle for Trondheim. British troops marching towards Oslo.

<u>The Thirty-third Week</u>     <u>April 22<sup>nd</sup> 1940</u>

Severe fighting in Norway. Germans bomb and machine-gun Allied troops incessantly. Sir John Simon announces his second war budget. German forces, marching south from Trondheim and north from Oslo are trying to link their forces. R.A.F. fighter planes in Norway. War Council meets. There is great criticism of the government.

## The Thirty-fourth Week    April 29th 1940

More Allied troops have landed in Norway.
British retreating North and South of Trondheim. Two
British submarines H.M.S. TARPON and H.M.S. STARLET are
reported lost. Allied troops retreating in Southern
Norway. German bombers crashes at Clacton.
There are new attacks on Narvik. Government criticism
continues. Italian fleet out on manoeuvres.

## The Thirty-fifth Week    May 10th 1940

## GERMANY INVADES HOLLAND BELGIUM AND LUXEMBURG on May 10th 1940.

Nazi troops crossed Belgian frontier. Hundreds of
parachute troops dropped. German planes bomb
open towns. Franco-British army rushing to the
help of the Low Countries. Many places in France
are bombed. On the Belgian front the customs barriers
are torn up. Mr. Chamberlain resigns. Mr. Churchill

31

is to be the new Prime Minister. 100 tpt German planes brought down over Holland, and 10 over Belgium. Some of the places in the Government are:-

Mr. Churchill, Lord Halifax (Foreign Minister) Mr. Chamberlain (Lord President of the Council) Mr. Attlee (Lord Privy Seal) Mr. Arthur Greenwood (Minister Without Portfolio) Sir John Simon (Lord Chancellor). Sir Kingsley Wood (Chancellor of the Exchequer) Lord Lloyd (Colonial Secretary) Mr. Herbert Morrison (Minister of Supply). Mr. Duff Cooper (Minister of Information). Mr. L. S. Amery (Secretary of State for India). Mr. M. Macdonald (Minister of Health). Lord Woolton (Minister of Food.) Mr. E. Bevin (Minister of Labour and National Service. Sir. A. Sinclair (Air Minister) Mr. A. V. Alexander (First Lord of the Admiralty. Dutch forces checking German advance. Germans attack French positions simultaneously Holland's defences have been penetrated at many points. Fighting continues in Rotterdam. German armoured columns have penetrated the Albert Canal defences 2,000 tanks have joined in battle near Tongres. Queen

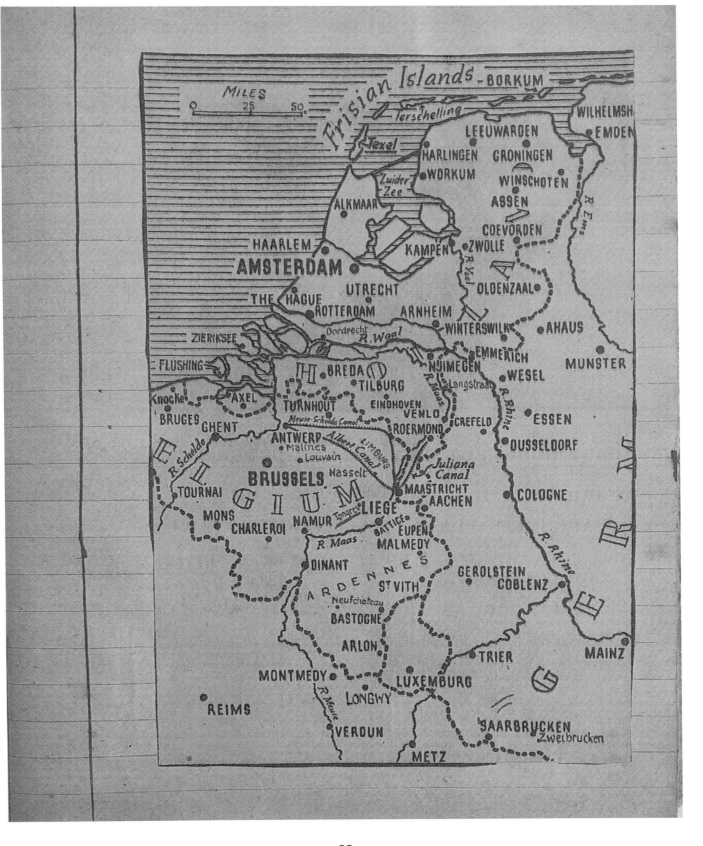

Wilhelmina has arrived in London with the Prime Minister of Holland. The Battle of the Meuse has begun. Germans have reached the Meuse from Liege to Namur and Sedan. Desperate fighting near Dinant. General Winkelman, C-in-C of the Dutch army has told them the army to lay down their arms. A volunteer force is being formed in Britain to deal with enemy parachute troops.

---

The Thirty-sixth Week.        May 15th 1940

German troops thrust back south of Sedan. German tank columns have made three breaches in the line between Namur and Sedan, and have started to fan out. Germans have crossed the Meuse, making a wide pocket. B.E.F. have withdrawn to positions west of Brussels. Brussels is in German hands. The Bulge grows larger. Germans attack towards St. Quentin and the Channel ports.

---

The Thirty-sixth Week.        May 21st. 1940.

Germans occupy Arras and Amiens, and Abbeville.

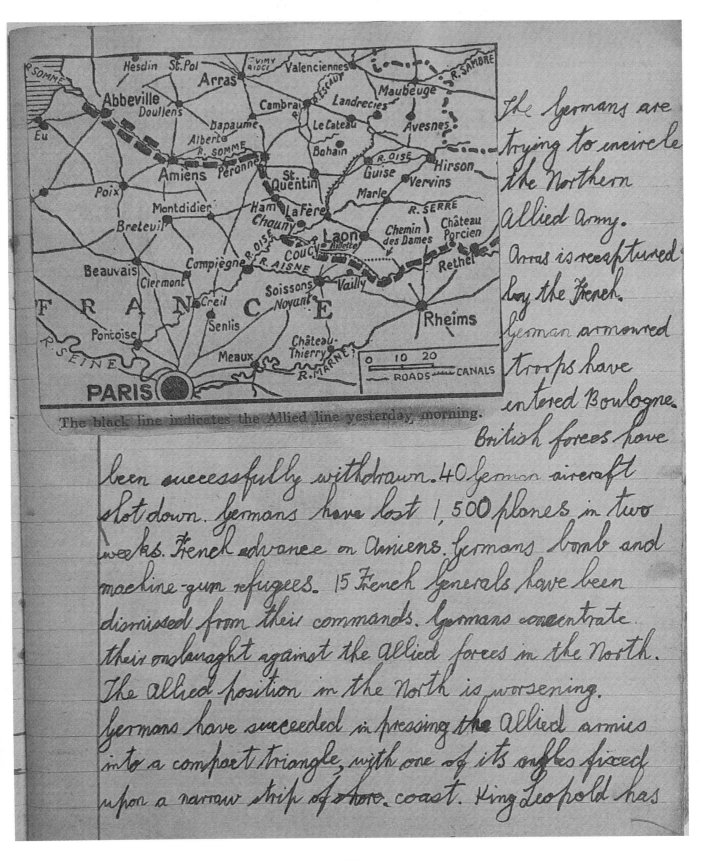

The black line indicates the Allied line yesterday morning.

The Germans are trying to encircle the Northern Allied Army. Arras is recaptured by the French. German armoured troops have entered Boulogne. British forces have been successfully withdrawn. 40 German aircraft shot down. Germans have lost 1,500 planes in two weeks. French advance on Amiens. Germans bomb and machine-gun refugees. 15 French Generals have been dismissed from their commands. Germans concentrate their onslaught against the Allied forces in the North. The Allied position in the North is worsening. Germans have succeeded in pressing the Allied armies into a compact triangle, with one of its angles fixed upon a narrow strip of shore coast. King Leopold has

35

told the Belgians to lay down their arms. As night falls the B.E.F. is in tighest corner of any Army in history

## The Thirty-seventh Week.

A big part was played by the Royal Navy in the battle. Motor torpedo boats made a perilous journey by canal to Amsterdam where the ratings set fire to the great oil stores thus preventing them from falling into the hands of the enemy

No deed was more heroic than that in which a Belgian officer sacrificed his life. To check the Nazi advance he blew up the important bridge at Maastricht which remained still intact when the enemy reached it

# The Thirty-eighth Week

R.A.F. screening retreat by bombing and machine-gunning enemy troops and mechanized-columns. Since May 10th the Germans have lost £5000 planes. Narvik has fallen to Allied forces. The B.E.F. is being successfully evacuated from Dunkirk Germans have lost

Systematic bombing by the R.A.F. of the roads along which the Nazis were bringing up reinforcements caused serious loss of life and disorganization. Here a British bomber is attacking a Nazi mechanized column on way to front

77 planes in 24 hours. Italy's attitude becomes more menacing. Lord Gort returns to London from France. The epic rear-guard action of the Northern Armies is

During the great battle, the Royal Air Force by its skill, initiative and courage proved that heavy odds could not prevent it from establishing a strong superiority over the Nazi planes. Here "Hurricanes" slash into Junkers "Ju 87's"

nearly finished. Paris is raided for an hour. 2,000 bombs are dropped. 254 people are killed and 652 injured. B.E.F. have lost 30,000 men killed, wounded, and missing. 335,000 of the B.E.F. have been brought out of Flanders.

The Thirty-ninth Week          June 5th 1940

Germans thrusting towards Paris. Germans have straddled the Oise-Aisne canal, and are fanning out to strike at key-points, near Amiens, Peronne, and Laon. They have seized the

the road through Soissons to Paris. M. Daladier
disappears disappears entirely. M. Reynaud takes over
the Ministry of Foreign Affairs. Germans have employed
2000 tanks today. Italy makes preparations for
war. A band of 12 miles round the coast of Italy,
Albania, and Italian overseas possessions is
announced dangerous to shipping. French have destroyed
400 German tanks since the offensive began. They have made
some strategic withdrawals. Germans bringing up strong
reinforcements. Italian ships are ordered to neutral ports.
The first V.C. of the war is awarded to Captain B.A.W.
Warburton-Lee, of the destroyer HARDY, who gave his life
in the heroic raid on Narvik on April 10th. Germans have
launch a new attack on a 60 mile front from Aumale
to Noyon. They have hurled 4,000 tanks and 1,000,000
men into the action. The French line reels back on
the Aumale-Noyon line. The Germans have attacked
from the sea to Montmédy with 2,000,000 men, and 3,500
tanks. They are within 50 miles of Paris. Fresh British
troops have been landed in France. Narvik has

been evacuated. The Admiralty announce the loss of the aircraft-carrier GLORIOUS, the transport ORAMA, the tanker OIL-PIONEER, and the destroyers, ACARTA and ARDENT, in a naval engagement off Norway.

ITALY declares war on Britain and France on June 10th.

The French withdraw to positions south of the Marne. French Government leaves Paris. Libya and Italian East Africa have been raided by the R.A.F. Malta is bombed by the Italians. Fighting is reported in Somaliland. Princess Juliana and her children arrive in Canada. Admiralty announces nine areas dangerous to shipping in the Mediterranean.

<u>The Fortieth Week.</u>      <u>June 12th, 1940</u>
Germans are within 20 miles of Paris. On the lower Oise they German armoured divisions smash their way to Persan and Beaumont. Further east they cross the great defence line of the Marne,

near Château-Thierry. On the Lower Seine, near between Rouen and Vernon, and around the city of Rheims the pressure increases hourly. Le Havre north of the Seine is in peril. A new B.E.F. has been sent across to France. Paris is occupied by the Germans. The German battleship SCHARNHORST has been bombed in Trondheim by the Fleet Air Arm. H.M.S. SCOTSTOUN (17,046 tons) has been torpedoed and sunk by a U-boat. German advance continues. British troops have captured Fort Capuzzo and Maddalena. Soviet troops have entered Lithuania. The British cruiser H.M.S. CALYPSO (4,180 tons) has been sunk by an Italian submarine. Russian troops enter Latvia. M. Reynaud has resigned and has been succeeded by M. Petain. Petain government of France has stopped fighting. Hitler and Mussolini had a four-hour talk at Munich. 100 Italian planes have been shot down since the war began. B.E.F. have been successfully withdrawn from France. 3 plenipotentiaries have been dispatched by M. Petain to meet Hitler's representatives.

# The Forty-first Week     June 20th 1940

Air raid on Britain. The armed merchant cruiser
H.M.S. ANDANIA (13,950 tons) was torpedoed and sunk
by a U-boat. N. Z. and A. troops have arrived in
Britain. The French plenipotentiaries have received
the German terms. R.A.F planes have bombed aerodromes in
Germany, and aeroplane factories at Turin and
Genoa, in Italy. The SCHARNHORST has been torpedoed and
bombed off Trondheim.
The British trawler MOONSTONE attacked an Italian submarine and forced it to surrender. France has

Principal bases of the Italian navy are on sides of the "boot." Advanced operating bases are on the heel and toe

On the Libyan coast Italy has naval bases at Benghazi and Tobruk. On the Red Sea coast of Eritrea is Massawa

VENICE TRIESTE
GENOA POLA
SPEZIA
ZARA
ANCONA
ITALY
MADDELENA
NAPLES CATTARO
BARI
BRINDISI
CAGLIARI TARANTO
MESSINA
CATANIA
PANTELLARIA

BENGHAZI
TOBRUK RHODES
LIBYA
EGYPT
RED SEA
MASSAWA
ERITREA

agreed to the armistice terms. General de Gaulle is to be the leader of all free Frenchmen. The Italian terms for an armistice were handed to the French plenipotentiaries near Rome. France stops fighting with Germany and Italy on June 24. German raiders crossed the British coast and 5 were shot down. British forces have landed at various points on the French coast. Much useful information was obtained.

---

## The Forty-second Week      June 27th 1940

Russia demands the surrender of Bessarabia and Bukovina from Rumania. Red troops have started to enter Bessarabia and Bukovina. The channel islands have been demilitarised. An Italian destroyer has been sunk and Italy has lost 9 submarines since the war began. Marshal Balbo, Governor-General and c-in-c in Libya, has been killed during a flight. M. Reynaud is in a critical condition following injuries received in a motor accident. German troops

have begun to occupy the Channel Islands. The
SCHARNHORST has again been heavily damaged by aircraft
of the Bomber Command. The liner ARANDORA STAR (15,500 tons)
has been torpedoed and sunk by a U-boat. The ship
was carrying 1,500 German and Italian internees to
Canada

## The Forty-third Week          July 4th, 1940

AIR MARSHAL: Balbo

Nearly two-thirds of the French Fleet is in
British hands. A British battle-squadron
attacked the French fleet at Oran, because
it did not surrender. F.A.A. bombed the
French battle-cruiser DUNKERQUE which was
beached after the Oran action. R.A.F. have laid a vast
minefield from the Baltic to the Northern tip of Norway.
The British submarine SNAPPER has sunk torpedoed 5 enemy
supply ships off the coast of Norway. Royal Navy have
taken action against the French battleship RICHELIEU.
Tea is to be rationed. Italian naval forces hastily retreated
when encountered by British warships. Eire has increased
her army by 100,000. R.A.F. shot 14 enemy planes

## The Forty-forth Week

French liberty murdered. A British naval squadron makes contact with a strong force of the Italian fleet and seeks an engagement. The Italians retire. Sea evacuation postponed. Japanese cabinet resigns. 140 Nazi raiders in down in a week.

**MARSHAL PETAIN,** President of the Council (Premier), eighty-four years old, hero of Verdun, later C.-in-C. of Army, Secretary of War 1934

## The Forty-fifth Week July 17th

Under pressure from Japan Britain agrees to close the Burma Road. H.M.S. VANDYCK employed as a naval auxiliary, has been sunk by air attack off the coast of Norway. The destroyer IMOGEN has been sunk as a result of a collision in dense fog. Lieut.-General

FASTEST CRUISER.—The Italian cruiser Bartolomeo Colleoni, claimed to be the fastest in the world, was sunk to the north west of Crete in action with H.M.A.S. Sydney and a small destroyer force. She is shown in the upper picture and the Sydney in the lower.

Sir Alan Brooke has been appointed C.-in-C Home

British

Forces. Since June 18th 476 civilians have been injured and 336 killed. Lithuania unites with Russia, while Latvia and Estonia follow suit. The submarine SALMON is overdue and must be presumed lost. H.M.S. BRAZEN has been lost. A minefield has been laid from North Cornwall to the coast of Eire.

Sir Kingsley Wood announces the War Emergency Budget.

The British liner LANCASTRIA (16,243 tons) was sunk off St. Nazaire on June 17th. The sinking of the French merchant ship Meknes was also announced. In the biggest attack on channel shipping to date, Germany lost 28 planes. 9 German motor-torpedo boats joined in the fight. They fled when attacked by two British destroyers and 2 motor torpedo boats. German planes numbering 80 launched an attack on Dover. The first army V.C.'s were awarded to Lieutenant H.M. Ervine-Andrews and

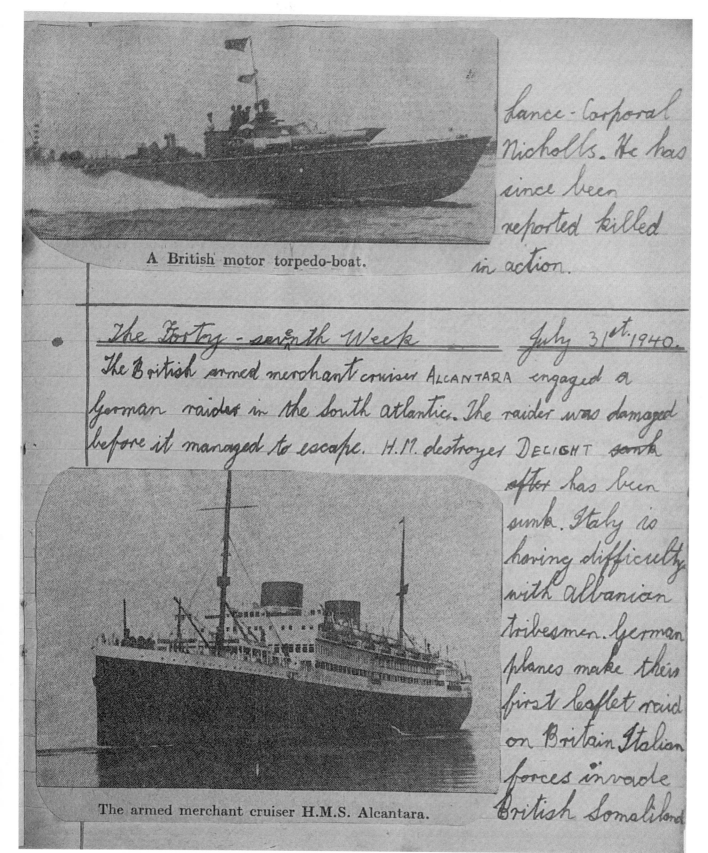

A British motor torpedo-boat.

Lance-Corporal Nicholls. He has since been reported killed in action.

## The Forty-seventh Week                    July 31st. 1940.

The British armed merchant cruiser ALCANTARA engaged a German raider in the South Atlantic. The raider was damaged before it managed to escape. H.M. destroyer DELIGHT sunk after has been sunk. Italy is having difficulty with Albanian tribesmen. German planes make their first leaflet raid on Britain Italian forces invade British Somaliland

The armed merchant cruiser H.M.S. Alcantara.

from Abyssinia. The British liner ACCRA (9,337 tons) has been sunk.

The Forty-eigth Week — Aug. 8th 1940

R.A.F. shoot down 76 enemy planes. Italians occupy Hargeisa, Odweina, and Zeila. The submarine OSWALD has been lost. The submarine ODIN has been lost. Revolt has broken out in Albania. 3 Australian Cabinet Ministers have been killed in an Air crash. The armed merchant cruiser TRANSYLVANIA (16,923 tons) has been sunk.

The Forty-ninth Week — Aug. 13th 1940

59 parachutes are dropped in town and villages in the Midlands, the North-East coast and Scotland. They are presumably to cause panic. R.A.F. raid Milan and Turin. The Greek cruiser HELLE is torpedoed by an unknown submarine. Italian troops concentrate on the Albanian-Greek frontier. The submarine ORPHEUS has been lost. The small British force

in Somaliland has evacuated it. 508 German planes have been shot down during the week (1) Germans down (2) British down (3) British pilots safe.

| | (1) | (2) | (3) |
|---|---|---|---|
| Awst 11 | 66 | 26 | 24 |
| Awst 12 | 62 | 13 | 12 |
| Awst 13 | 78 | 13 | 3 |
| Aws 14 | 31 | 7 | 5 |
| Awst 15 | 180 | 34 | 17 |
| Awst 16 | 75 | 22 | 8 |
| Awst 17 | — | — | — |
| Awst 18 | 153 | 22 | 10 |
| Awst 19 | 6 | 3 | 1 |
| Awst 20 | 7 | 2 | 1 |
| Awst 21 | 13 | 1 | — |
| Awst 22 | 10 | 4 | 2 |
| Awst 23 | 4 | — | — |
| Awst 24 | 50 | 19 | 7 |
| Awst 25 | 54 | 13 | 10 |
| Awst 26 | 47 | 15 | 4 |
| Awst 27 | 4 | — | — |
| Awst 28 | 28 | 14 | 1 |
| Awst 29 | 11 | — | — |
| Awst 30 | 62 | 25 | 15 |
| Awst 31 | 85 | 37 | 12 |
| Total | 1026 | 267 | 138 |

## The Fiftieth Week     Aug. 20th 1940

Britain will give a 99 year lease of bases in Newfoundland and the West Indies to the U.S.A. Leon Trotsky turbulent exile from Russia, is murdered at tea by a friend. R.A.F. bombers have bombed Germany and German-occupied territory, also the Caproni aircraft works in at Milan, and the Fiat works at Turin. German guns shell a convoy in the Channel, and Dover. R.A.F. attack the guns for 6 hours. London is raided. Eire is bombed by a German aircraft. R.A.F. bomb Berlin. The destroyer HOSTILE and submarine SPEARFISH are lost.

## The Fifty-first Week.     Aug. 28th

Trouble between Rumania and Hungary.

French Equatorial Africa and Chad Territory said that they would continue the war with Britain. 62 German planes brought down during raids on this country. Our bombers bombed military objectives in Germany. Rumania surrendered 20,000 sq. miles of territory to Hungary. Berlin bombed. British evacuee ship torpedoed. All were saved. —

First anniversary of the outbreak of War.

America gave us 50 old destroyers in exchange for naval Bases in the West Indies. Iron Guardists fired shots at the Palace at Bucharest. The V.C. was awarded posthumous to Acting Leading Seaman Jack Mantle of H.M.S. FOYLE BANK. R.A.F. bombed Berlin arms works. Germans launched mass attacks against London. 109 Germans down. Rumania's Premier M. Gigurtu has resigned, and General Ion Antonescu is to be the new Premier.

Second-Lieutenant Annand, V.C.

A Messerschmitt 109 fighter plane shot down on the South-East Coast of England.

<u>The Fifty-second Week</u>          <u>Sept. 5th 1940</u>

British cruisers shelled Scarpanto in the Dodecanese Islands. King Carol gave General Antonescu full dictorial powers. Hungarian troops marched into Transylvania. 4,000 German troops were drowned when the transport MARION was torpedoed. King Carol of Rumania abdicated in favour of his 18-year-old son Michael. The submarine TRUANT has rescued the captain and crew of a British merchant ship. Germans raid London. 306 people were killed, and 1,300 seriously injured. Lance-Corporal Harry Nicholls, is alive, but a prisoner in Germany. Ex-King Carol arrived in

Switzerland. German artillery shelled Dover. British guns fired back. The submarines RORQUAL and OSIRIS between them sank 3 supply ships. R.A.F. bombed Berlin.

## The Fifty-third Week. Sept. 11th 1940

London bombed. 90 Germans down. Buckingham Palace raided. Egypt has been attacked. 185 Germans down. Berlin bombed. The bomb which menaced St. Paul's has been dug out. It weighed over a ton. It was Lieut. R. Davies who dug it out. The Tate Gallery and Chancery Court were damaged during recent raids.

## The Fifty-fourth Week. Sept. 17th

In the first half of this month 2,000 civilians were killed and 8,000 wounded. R.A.F. raided invasion ports. The submarine STURGEON sank an enemy troop-ship. German barges bombed. These were already full of troops. London bombed.

Japan invades French Indo-China. 294 people, including
83 children were lost when a British liner was
torpedoed. The King announces that the creation
of the George Cross and Medal for civilians.

## The Fifty-fifth Week.         Sept. 24

De Gaulle's envoys were sent in an attempt to
win Dakar, but were fired on, and withdrew. Berlin
raided heavily for 4 hours. 26 Germans down during
raids on London. 100 French planes bomb Gibraltar.
The submarines TUNA and H 49 have sunk supply
ships. America bans the export of iron and steel
scrap except to Britain and the Western Hemisphere.
America makes a loan of 25 million dollars to China.
Germany, Italy, and Japan have signed a 10 year
military pact. 133 Germans down. The first flotilla
of U.S. destroyers have arrived. R.A.F. bomb
military objectives in Germany.

## The Fifty-sixth Week.

Oct. 1st 1940

Four-hour raid on Berlin. Berlin children being evacuated. 10 Germans down. Government reshuffle. Chamberlain resigns. Hitler and Mussolini meet at the Brenner Pass. Greece is threatened. Sir Charles Portal, chief of Bomber Command, becomes Chief of Staff instead of Sir Cyril Newall who is to be Governor-General of New Zealand. Sir Richard Pierse new Bomber Chief. 2,549 German planes down since war began. We lost 672 machines with 324 pilots saved. 700 major raids on Germany. Trade Union Council meets.

## The Fifty-seventh Week.

Oct. 8th 1940

30,000 German troops enter Rumania. 250,000 Italian troops on the Greek-Albanian frontier. Burma Road to re-open on Oct. 17th. It was an accident that French war-ships were allowed to pass through the straights of Gibraltar. London has its longest night raid. Navy bombards Cherbourg. St. Paul's Cathedral

56

has been bombed. De Gaulle arrived in the Cameroons. R. AF. bomb military objectives in Germany. Germans have lost 2,641 planes over Britain.

## The Fifty-eigth Week                    Oct. 15th 40

London has its worst night raid. H.M.S. Ajax has sunk two Italian destroyers and crippled a third. 4 Italian merchant-men have been torpedoed. Navy bombard Dunkirk. War costs £9,000,000 a day. A German convoy has been sunk. H.M.S. Liverpool which was damaged recently is safely in port. Kiel was bombed. Vice-Admiral John C. Tovey becomes Commander-in-Chief of the Home Fleet. Sir Henry Harwood becomes Lord Commissioner of the Admiralty. The Burma Road into China has been opened.

H.M.S. Ajax

During September air-raids on Britain 6,954 civilians were killed and 10,615 seriously. Yugoslavia has signed a trade agreement with Germany. Himmler arrives in Spain.

## The Fifty-ninth Week. Oct. 22nd 44

Hitler arrives in Paris. Berlin has its 22nd raid. 2 German supply ships have been torpedoed. An Italian destroyer has been sunk by H.M.S. KIMBERLEY. Hitler meets Franco. Himmler leaves Barcelona. Berlin bombed. 14 German planes down. A German torpedo-boat and an Italian supply ship have been torpedoed. Italian press reviving the anti-Greek campaign. Great activity among Italian troops in Albania. Germans lose eight planes.

A BRITISH WELLINGTON BOMBER

# ITALY INVADES GREEK.

<u>The Sixtieth Week</u>    <u>Oct. 29th 1940</u>

All aid for Greece. Berlin bombed. British
Navy has mined Greek waters, chiefly the Gulf of
Corinth. Greeks advance into Italy Albanian territory.
Greek army is estimated at 400,000. Naples
bombed for three-quarters of an hour. Greek
navy bombarded Italian positions. British troops
have landed at Crete. London had a night without
a single warning.

Raider attacked convoy <u>The Sixty-first Week</u>    <u>Nov. 5th 1940</u>
in Atlantic. Roosevelt is to be President for a third
term. Emden, Bremen, Bremerhaven, were bombed.
We have lent Greece £5,000,000. Lord Gort is
to be Inspector-General of the Home Guard.
R.A.F. have heavily bombed Brindisi in Italy
and the Krupps works in Germany. Turin and
Milan were heavily bombed. Mr. Chamberlain died

at the age of 72. The Greeks have surrounded
a crack Italian divison in the Pindus
mountains. A most violent earthquake occured in
Rumania which seriously damaged the oil refineries.
Molotov is on his way to Berlin.

## The Sixty-second Week.                    Nov. 12 1940

Hitler and Molotov had a conference in
Berlin. Fleet Air Arm aircraft attacked the Italian
Fleet at Taranto, crippling half of Italy's
battleship strength. Air Marshal Sir R. Brooke
-Popham has been appointed C-in-C, Far East.
The ashes of Mr. Neville Chamberlain were buried
in Westminster Abbey. The Greeks have launched

An Italian battleship of the Littorio class (35,000 tons), one of which has been badly dam[aged] by Fleet Air Arm planes.

This map shows the treble land-locked port of Taranto in the "heel" of Italy, where the Italian admirals thought their ships would be safe. They felt certain that no attack by sea was possible, for submarines cannot get through the channel between the mercantile port and the outer harbour. The ingenuity of our Navy beat them, for we used the new technique of torpedo attack by the Fleet Air Arm. The positions at which various Italian ships were hit are indicated on the map. Two nights later Taranto was bombed again, as admitted by the Italian communique of Nov. 14.

a new offensive along the whole front. Places in Germany bombed heavy. The Egyptian Prime Minister died at the opening of Parliament in Cairo. R.A.F. bombed Lorient in Brittany. 34 ships got safely home after their convoy had been attacked by a raider in the Atlantic. Greeks captured objectives near Koritza. Acting Captain E. S. Fogarty Fegen of the JERVIS BAY has been awarded the V. C. Gabun is under de Gaulle's control. British light forces bombarded Mogadishu, main port of Italian Somaliland. Severe night raids on the Midlands. Hungary has joined the Axis. Britain is to get 46 American "Flying Fortress" bombers. The Skoda Works in Czechosl -ovakia were bombed.

## The Sixty - third Week.    Nov. 21$^{st}$ 1940

The Greeks have captured Koritza. R.A.F. bombed Duisberg - Ruhort. It is the greatest inland port in the world. The plane carrying Air Marshal Boyd was forced down in Sicily and he was interned. 7 Italian planes were shot down over the Straits of Dover. Greek forces continue to advance. Enemy aircraft severely bombed a town in the West. Viscount Craigavon, Prime Minister of N. Ireland, died suddenly. Slovakia joined the Axis. R.A.F. R.A.F. continuously bombing the Italians. The Italian Navy were observed in the Mediterranean Sea and fled as soon as the British fleet endeavoured to make contact. 2 German supply ships were torpedoed. R.A.F. attacked many targets in Germany including Ghent, Rotterdam, Flushing, Antwerp, Calais and Boulogne. and Turin. Sabotage occured in Norway.

---

<u>The Sixty-fourth Week</u>.    <u>Nov. 28th 1940</u>

There was an attack on Argyrocastro. A state of emergency was proclaimed throughout Rumania. 7 Italian aircraft shot down. There was an engagement between British and German light naval forces in the Channel. H.M.S. JAVELIN was damaged. The Prime Minister celebrated his 66th birthday. Greeks captured Pogradets. The Greek destroyer EAGLE has sunk an Italian submarine. Southampton was the chief target for German bombers. America has lent China £25,000,000. During November 221 enemy planes were shot down. The British submarine TRIAD has been lost. Mr. J. Kennedy U.S. Ambassador to Britain has tendered his resignation to President Roosevelt. Southampton was the chief target for German bombers. British bombers bombed Wilhelmshaven, and Lorient. In Italy Naples, Catania, and Augusta were heavily bombed. Birmingham was the chief target for German bombers. There was more rioting in Norway. The war costs £13,000,000 a day. The Greeks captured Argyrocastro.

---

## The Sixty - fifth Week     Dec. 5

24 enemy planes destroyed. Dusseldorf

bombed for 12 hours. The Greeks occupied Santi Quaranta. Marshal Badoglio, Italian Chief of Staff, resigned. A south-west town bore the brunt of the German night raid. The British armed liner CARNARVON CASTLE (21,222 tons)

H.M.S. Carnarvon Castle.

has been in action with a German sea -raider in the South Atlantic. The German vessel succeeded in escaping. Another Italian Army chief was replaced. The Greeks have occupied Delvino. Two Generals of the Italian Air Force were killed in a plane crash. Three more Italian officers of high rank have been replaced. A Nazi sea-raider was again engaged by the British cruiser ENTERPRISE (9,000 tons). London.

was the chief
target for German
night raiders. There
was a large fire

in the Rumanian oil zone. General Wavell
has captured Sidi Barani together with 6,000
prisoners and three generals. Since her entry into
the war Italy has lost 460 planes. A West
Midland town was heavily bombed. The War
Damage Bill has been issued. 2 spies were
hanged at Pentonville Prison.

The Sixty-fifth Week                    Dec. 12th 1940

20,000 Italian prisoners have been captured in
Libya. The German ship RHEIN has been captured
in the West Indies. 30,000 Italian prisoners
have been captured in Libya. The Greeks are
pushing forward towards Berat and Elbasan.
The British submarine SUNFISH has sunk a
German supply-ship. The King reached the age

of 45. Marshal Petain has dismissed Pierre Laval, Foreign Minister, and Pierre Flandin has been appointed in his place. The Italians are still forced to retreat into Libya. A part of Tepelini has been set on fire by the Italians. The meat ration is to be reduced from 2/2d to 1/1d worth per person. A serious fire broke out in the Rumanian oilfields, at Ploesti. 26 Italian planes shot down. Five Polish pilots were awarded the D.F.C. Our forces captured Sollum and Fort Capuzzo. Greek forces have captured Tepelini. At night towns in the Midlands were the chief target. Britain has asked America for financial assistance.

## The Sixty-sixth Week Dec. 17th 1940

President Roosevelt outlined a new plan for giving aid to Britain. There are new aircraft called Whirlwinds. Mechanised units, launched a formidable attack on the outer defences of Bardia. Shipping losses week ending Dec. 8-9 were 101,190 tons. A German spy Charles Van Den Kieboom was executed at Pentonville Prison. Army, Navy, and R.A.F. combine in fierce attack on Bardia. The Greeks are still mainting pressure on the Italians. Britain purchased 16 ships from the U.S. During fighting in Libya we lost only 72 killed and 738 wounded. Italian prisoners number 31,546. Bardia has been completely encircled by our forces. Mannheim and Milan have been bombed. British forces penetrated the outer defences of Bardia. Valona has been shelled by our naval forces. Merseyside was the main target for German raiders. Bardia is in flames. Liverpool was the main target for German bombers. Lord Halifax is to be British Ambassador to America, and Capt. Margesson becomes War Secretary. There were

A view of the roof of the west corridor of St. George's Hall, Liverpool, where courts and robing-room were destroyed during a recent raid.

heavy night raids on Manchester and Liverpool. R.A.F. heavily bombed Venice. Winston Churchill broadcast to the Italian people.

## The Sixty-seventh Week          Dec 2 4 1940

Tripoli, in Libya, has been heavily bombed by the R.A.F. Italian aerodromes have been also bombed. R.A.F. bombed Rhineland and Dunkirk, Boulogne and Ostend. Enemy raiders concentrated over towns in Lancashire. The King broadcasted to the Empire. Dec. 25th Christmas Day. Boxing Day was not a Bank Holiday. The Greeks continue to advance. Our aircraft bombed the U-boat base at Lorient. Enemy raiders concentrated their attack against a town in south-west Britain.

The Greek submarine PAPANICOLAS has torpedoed 3 Italian supply-ships. German planes showered thousands of incendiary bombs on London. The attack was a deliberate attempts to set fire to the city. The Guildhall Hall was destroyed, nine churches hospitals, many homes and commercial buildings The British destroyer ACHERON has been lost. In the Western Desert 38,114 Italian prisoners have been taken. R.A.F. bombers On Christmas Day a German pocket battleship tried to attack a British convoy in the North Atlantic but was chased by a British

DEC. 29. 1940

Debris in the main Banqueting Hall of Guildhall, gutted by Nazi fire bombs.

Naval force including H.M.S BERWICK (10,000 ton cruiser).

H.M.S. Berwick

R.A.F. bombers bomb -ed Naples and Valona. British forces around Bardia continue to shell the town. The Greeks continue to advance. Up to January, 1941 Britain will have 4,500,000 men under arms. The Government are to conscript men for fire-watching. R.A.F bombers attacked Taranto, Naples, and Palermo. The Raf heavily attacked Bremen. An unidentified plane dropped bombs on Eire.

The Sixty-eighth Week.                    Jan. 2 1940
The R.A.F. again heavily bombed Bremen and and the invasion ports. German raiders concentrated on Cardiff. German squadrons have arrived in Italy. The Australians have penetrated a sector of the defences of Bardia. The British submarine THUNDERBOLT, has sunk an Italian submarine. This submarine was.

originally the THETIS. President Roosevelt is announced that he is Mr. Harry Hopkins his personal representative to England. The meat ration has been reduced from 1/10 to 1/6. The attack on Bardia continues. Our troops have broken through the defence to a depth of two miles on a front of nine miles. Bremen was raided for three nights. 20,000 fire bombs were dropped. Bardia has surrendered. 30,000 prisoners were captured including 3 Generals. The British forces in Libya are driving on toward Tobruk. Miss Amy Johnson, was drowned when her plane crashed in the Thames Estuary.

Mechanized British forces have reached Tobruk. 94,000 Italians have been captured in Libya. Tobruk has been completely

GENERAL MACKAY, who is in command of the Australian force which penetrated the Bardia defences.

MISS AMY JOHNSON

encircled. Lord Baden-Powell has died in Kenya at the age of 83. There has been rioting in Norway.

## The Sixty-ninth Week          Jan. 9th 1941

British forces continue to mass around Tobruk. Emden and Wikhelmshaven were heavily raided. Greeks continue to advance slowly. Sir Archibald Sinclair, Air Minister, announced a scheme to train boys over 16 for entry into the Air Force. A few bombs were dropped on Dublin. R.A.F carried a sweep across across Northern France. There were 100 fighters as escort. Naples was heavily bombed. Portsmouth was heavily bombed. British forces in Kenya have captured El Wak and Buna. The Greeks captured Klisura. Germans showered large numbers of incendiary bombs on London. 44,800 Italian prisoners were captured at Bardia. Amlwch was machine-gunned by an enemy raider. on Nobody was wounded or killed. / January 12th.

Mr. Wendell Wilkie is coming to England.
British fighters machine-gunned Nazi troops
in France. Portsmouth was again the main

The cruiser Southampton

target for the German raiders. British artillery
were in action against the defences of Tobruk.
German dive-bombers bombed our fleet
in the Sicilian Channel. 12 bombers were
shot down. The aircraft-carrier ILLUSTRIOUS
and the cruiser SOUTHAMPTON were damaged.
The latter had to be sunk because she was

damaged severely. The destroyer H.M.S. GALLANT was also lost. British bombers raided Catania in Sicily. Week ending January 5 only 4 British ships were lost. Preparations around Tobruk are continuing. Nearly all Abyssinia is seething with revolt. Two enemy night bombers were destroyed over Britain by our fighters.

## The Seventieth Week Jan 16<sup>th</sup> 1941

The R.A.F. raided Catania in Sicily and destroyed 35 enemy planes. Bristol was the main objective of the enemy night raiders. R.A.F. bombed Wilhelmshaven. The British Submarine PANDORA sank 2 Italian supply-ships. Swansea was the main target for the night raiders. During attacks on Malta ten enemy dive-bombers were shot down. The Greek submarine PROTEUS. has sunk an Italian supply-ship. British forces have recaptured Kassala and penetrated 15 miles into Eritrea. Our forces in Kenya have also taken the offensive. British troops broke through the inner and outer defences of Tobruk. The Italian cruiser SAN GIORGIO was set ablaze. Rioting has broken out in Bucharest. The DAILY WORKER and THE WEEK have been suppressed by the Home Secretary. Greeks have occupied heights around Klisura. Tobruk has been captured. Two day raiders have been shot down. The R.A.F. carried out two daylight sweeps over enemy-occupied territory. Mr. Wendell Wilkie left New York for London. Rumania was in a state of civil war.

### The Seventy-first Week     Jan 23rd 44

Prisoners taken at Tobruk numbered 20,000. Lord Halifax, our new Ambassador to America, arrived at Cheapsake Bay aboard the new battleship KING GEORGE V. In Libya our forces are advancing towards Derna. General Antonescu has crushed the revolt in Rumania. In Libya our forces are 120 miles West of Tobruk. London has had

no raids for six nights. British troops in Libya have encircled Derna. In Eritrea w Our forces have attacked Libya, Eritrea, Abyssinia and Italian Somaliland. The Greeks have repelled a number of Italian counter-attacks. British forces in Eritrea are closing round Agordat. Free French forces raided Murzuk in Southern Libya. We lost 11 ships through enemy action for week ending Jan 19. Bomba has been completely smashed by the R.A.F. H.M. Submarine TRITON has been lost. Naples has been heavily raided by the R.A.F. Youths of 18 and 19 and men from 37 to 40 are to be called up.

---

## The Seventy-second Week          Jan 30.

After hard fighting our troops have

occupied Derna. In Eritrea, our tanks cut the road linking Agordat and Barentu. The R.A.F carried out a heavy raid against Tripoli. Greek pressure on Tepelini is increasing. 400 American bombers have been flown over the Atlantic so far. Our troops have captured Agordat. The enemy are in full retreat in Italian Somaliland. British forces in Eritrea have captured Barentu. Fleet Air Arm planes torpedoed and bombed the Tirso Dam in Sardinia. British forces in Libya have captured Cyrene. In Eritrea, our forces are active around Keren. R.A.F. bombers, escorted by fighters, swept over Northern France. In Africa 24 Italian planes were captured or destroyed on the ground.

MILES
0   50   100
ROADS
RAILWAY

ERITREA

Kassala
Biscia
Agordat
Keren
Asmara
Massawa
Zula
Mogolo
Barentu
Adi Ugri
Adi Caie
Ducambia
Adi Quala
Umm Hagar
Entiscio
Aksum
Biacuna
Adowa
Makalle
WALKAIT
ANGLO-EGYPTN SUDAN
ATBARA
Gallabat
Metemma
Gondar
ABYSSINIA
ADDIS ABABA
N

MEDITERRANEAN SEA
Apollonia
Derna
Cyrene
Martuba
Benghazi
Barce
Bomba
Benina
Tobruk
Berka
Mechili
Soluch
Magrun
CYRENAICA
El Gubbi
Agedabia
MILES
0   50   100
1ST Class Roads
2ND RAILWAYS
Hasseiat

78

## The Seventy-Third Week                Feb 6th 1941

In Libya our forces are continuing their
advance on Benghazi. In Eritrea they are
closing round Keren. Mr. J. G. Winant is to be
U.S. Ambassador to London. After a whirlwind
advance of 160 miles of rocky, mountainous
country, our troops captured BENGHAZI.

CAMPAIGN DIARY

Outstanding dates in General
Wavell's Libyan campaign are:
Dec. 9.—The Army sets out
     from Mersa Matruh.
Dec. 12.—Sidi Barrani captured.
Dec. 16.—Sollum captured.
Dec. 31.—British patrols near
     Tobruk.
Jan. 3.—Bardia attacked.
Jan. 4.—Bardia falls.
Jan. 7.—El Adem Aerodrome,
     Tobruk, abandoned
     by Italians.
Jan. 12.—Bomba seaplane base
     abandoned.
Jan. 22.—Tobruk captured.
Jan. 30.—Derna taken.
Feb. 3.—Cyrene and Apollonia
     evacuated by Italians.
Feb. 7.—Benghazi in our
     hands.

Our forces have occupied
El Agheila, 175 miles south of Benghazi.
The Greeks have thrown back an Italian
counter-attack in the Klisura area. Heavy
and light units of the Fleet bombarded
Genoa. Admiral Darlan is to be Vice
-Premier and Foreign Minister for the Vichy

Government. British forces in Eritrea are advancing down the Red Sea coast. Britain broke ~~out~~ off diplomatic relations with Rumania. R.A.F. have bombed the invasion ports. Lt.-Gen. Sir Henry Maitland Wilson has been promoted C-in-C Cyrenaica. Tension is increasing in Bulgaria. Free French Forces from Chad have taken several oasis in the Kufra area. 30,000 German troops disguised as tourists have arrived in Bulgaria. R.A.F. have bombed Catania and Comiso, in Sicily. Australian Air Forces have taken up stations in Northern Malaya.

---

## The Seventy-fourth Week Feb 13<sup>th</sup> 1941

British parachute troops have been dropped in the Apulia province of Italy. In Italian Somaliland our ~~forces~~ have captured Kismayu. The R.A.F. have heavily bombed the invasion ports. Kurmuk, in the Sudan, has been recaptured. The Italians have been forced to withdraw by the Greeks around Tepelini. The debate on the Lease-and-Lend Bill opened in the American Senate

ALREADY this new British plane, the Blackburn Botha I, is helping to fight the U-boat menace. Notable for its speed and manœuvrability, it can be used for reconnaissance, torpedo-carrying, or bombing. Dimensions: length, 60ft; span, 59ft; height, 18ft. And for defence it has a gun turret on top of the fuselage just behind the wings.

The shipping loses for the week ending Feb. 19th were 9 British and 4 allied ships. F.A.A. aircraft have sunk a 4,000 ton German-ship. Strong forces of bombers and fighters have been sent to strengthen the R.A.F. in the Far East. Italian counter-attacks in Albania have been repulsed by the Greeks with heavy losses.

The Seventy-fifth Week February 20th 1941

Mr. Anthony Eden, and General Sir

John Dill, C.I.G.S. have arrived in Cairo. Our troops in Italian Somaliland crossed the Juba River. South African troops captured Mega, in Abyssinia. The main target for German night raiders was Swansea. Mr. R. G. Menzies, Prime Minister of Australia, has arrived in this country. Swansea was again the main target of the enemy night raiders. Brest was heavily raided by the R.A.F. In Italian Somaliland our forces captured Jumbo. The 19-years-olds registered with the forces. In Abyssinia patriot forces have occupied Shogali. The R.A.F heavily raided Calais and Boulogne. Admiral Darlan has formed a new French cabinet of five. Marshal

Petain is still head of the state. Brava in Italian Somaliland has been captured. Mr. Eden and Sir John Dill left Cairo for Ankara. Our forces have captured Mogadishu, capital of Italian Somaliland. British bombers and fighters attacked German shipping during daylight. British forces have occupied the island of Castellorizo in the Dodecanese. The London area, a S.W. town and a S. Wales coast town were the chief targets of enemy night raiders.

<u>The Seventy-sixth Week.</u>     <u>Feb. 27th 1941</u>

In Italian Somaliland our forces are rounding up thousands of prisoners. The British troops had covered 570 miles in 13 days to capture Mogadishu. Cologne was heavily raided by the R.A.F. The raid was one of the fiercest of the war. British fighters shot down 26 Italian

aircraft over Southern Albania.
Bulgaria signed the Axis Pact in
Vienna, and German troops crossed into
Bulgaria. Our troops have strongly
attacked Keren. Ex - King Alfonso of
Spain died in Rome, aged 54. During
an attack on a convoy in the North
Sea by German E - boats the destroyer
EXMOOR was sunk. German troops have
reached Varna, in Bulgaria. Free French
forces captured Kufra, an oasis in South
Libya. Bardera, 120 miles north of Gelib,
in Italian Somaliland was captured by
our troops. Cologne was again heavily
raided by our bombers. German mechanised
forces swept through Bulgaria towards
Greece. Mr. Anthony Eden and General
Sir John Dill arrived in Athens. A
South Wales coastal town was the
chief objective of the Nazi night bombers.

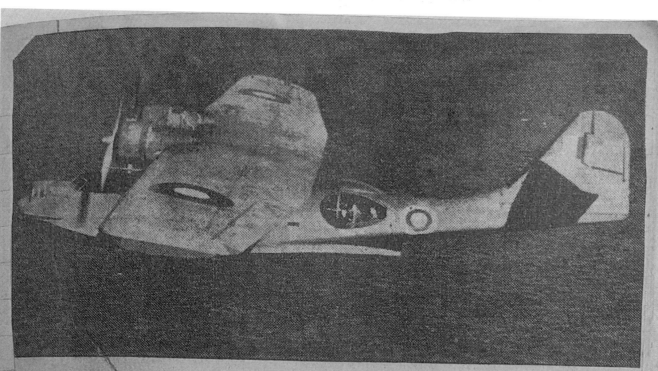

New protection for convoys: a Consolidated Catalina flying-boat of a new type now operating with the R.A.F. Coastal Command. These big planes have a very long range, and will be a formidable weapon in the Battle of the Atlantic.

Admiral Sir Andrew Cunnigham, General Sir Archibald Wavell, and Air Chief Marshal Sir Arthur Longmore were awared the G.C.B. by the King. Our losses in Italian Somaliland up to know are 52 killed, 151 wounded and 2 missing, while we captured in Africa 150,000 Italian prisoners. Summer-time is to be extended 2 hours from May 3 to August 9. Britain broke off relations with Bulgaria. Patriot forces in Abyssinia

have captured Burye and Mansuka.
At the King's request, Sunday, March
23 has been appointed a day of
national prayer.

## The Seventy-seventh Week. March 6 1941

Mr. Eden and General Sir John
Dill arrived in Cairo from Athens.
Many Norwegian patriots
and German prisoners were
landed from Lofoten Islands
at a British port. Eleven
German ships were sunk there
The oil tanks and fishing
factories were the main
objective. British forces occupied
Tet-Tet in Italian Somaliland. Mines
laid by the R.A.F and F.A.A. had
been responsible for the destruction
of 100 enemy transports. During a raid

on Malta 16 German aircraft were lost. H. M. destroyer DAINTY has been lost. London was the main objective of the enemy night raiders. The Italian submarine ANFITRITE has been sunk. The U.S. Senate passed the Lease-and-Lend Bill. Mr. Bevin, Minister of Labour, announced that all shipyards would pass under Government control. Relentless pressure on the Italians in North and South Abyssinia continues. The Italian commerce raider RAMB I has been sunk by the New Zealand cruiser LEANDER. Mr George Rendel, British Minister to Bulgaria, left Sofia for Istanbul. The R.A.F heavily bombed Boulogne. During the night raids on this country eight enemy aircraft were destroyed. An Italian cruiser of the CONDOTTIERI class has been torpedoed. Under pressure of Abyssinian patriots the

Italians fell back on Debra Marcos.
The American House of Representatives passed
the Lease - and - Lend Bill. Shipping losses
during the week ending March 2nd were
20 British ships. 8 allied and 1 neutral
An attempt on the life of Mr. George
Rendel was made. During the night
raids on this country 9 enemy aircraft
were destroyed. Fierce fighting continued
in the Tepelini area of Albania.

The Seventy-eighth Week  March 13th 1941
During the night's raids on this
country 13 enemy aircraft were shot down.
Violent fighting continued in the Tepelini
area of Albania. In Eritrea our troops
continued their gradual closing-
in movements on Keren. In
Italian Somaliland and Abyssinia
satisfactory progress was made

by our troops. The Italian losses in Albania had reached a total of at least 15,000. Admiral Sir Percy Noble was appointed C.-in-C. Western Approaches. The rationing of jam, marmalade, and syrup was announced. The ration will be 8 oz. per head per calendar month. From March 9 to March 15. 35 night raiders were shot down over this country. Mr. Ernest Bevin, Minister of Labour, announced that women aged 20 and 21, and men aged 41 and 42, who are not employed in certain important industries, will be required to register for work of national importance. The Italians have failed to break through the Greek line in Albania. British troops have recaptured Berbera, in capital of British Somaliland. Our troops in Eritrea heavily attacked Keren. Yugoslavia has asked Germany to guarantee the neutrality of Salonika. A fire broke out in the German liner BREMEN which caused serious damage. Our shipping losses for week ending March 9th. was 98,832 tons. The sinking of three U-boats was announced by the Navy. London was the target of the enemy night raiders. Mr. Eden met M. Sarajoglu, Turkish Foreign Minister at Cyprus to discuss the Balkan situation. Britain has asked for the use of U.S. Navy yards to repair warships. British and Indian forces made further advances in the struggle for Keren.

The Seventy - ninth Week. March 20th 1941.

The Admiralty announced the sinking of 5 Italian ships. Keren, in Eritrea was heavily attacked by our troops supported by dive - bombers. Plymouth was the main target of enemy night raiders. Jarabub, Italian oasis fort in Libyan Desert was captured by British troops. The SCHARNHORST and GNEISENAU, 26,000 ton German battle-cruisers, known to be at large in the Atlantic are being hunted by our naval units and aircraft. There are German demands on Yugoslavia. Our forces continue to fight their way onwards towards Keren. Yugoslavia has signed an agreement with Germany. There were demonstrations in many parts of Yugoslavia against Government's capitulation. Mr. Matsuoka, Japanese Foreign Minister arrived in Moscow to see M. Molotov before proceeding to Berlin. Six enemy planes have been destroyed during the week in night raids on this country. Berlin was heavily attacked by the R.A.F. Turkey and Russia said that if either be involved in a war, (the other can) each can count on the other's understanding and neutrality. British troops striking West from Jijiga captured vital pass.

on road to Addis Ababa. Men in age 37 class must register for service on April 12. Our losses in the African fighting up to Feb. 23 were 2,966, including 604 killed. Italian casualties were over 200,000 of whom 180,000 were prisoners. Merchant shipping losses for week ending March 16-17 were 71,773 tons. Mr. Matsuoka arrived in Berlin. The submarine STURGEON has sunk an enemy tanker. Our forces continue to draw in on Keren, while the South Africans make satisfactory progress towards Harar.

<u>The Eightieth Week</u>       <u>March 27<sup>th</sup> 1941.</u>

A military coup in Yugoslavia resulted in a complete change of government. The Regent, Prince Paul was displaced, and 17-year old King Peter was set at the head of his country. The ministers who signed the Axis Pact were detained. General Dusan Simovitch became

PRINCE PAUL

Prime Minister. Keren, key to all Eritrea, and Harar were both captured. The British forces in Eritrea are pursuing the Italians along the road to Asmara. Mobilisation continued in Jugoslavia. Air raid casualties to date amongst civil population in Britain stated to be, 28,859 killed 40,166 seriously wounded. There has been an engagement between the British and Italian Fleets in the Eastern Mediterranean. Our fleet included the battleships, WARSPITE, VALIANT, and BARHAM, the aircraft-carrier FORMIDABLE, the cruisers ORION, AJAX, GLOUCESTER and PERTH; and a number of destroyers. The Italian Fleet included the battleship VITTORIO VENETO; and two battleships of the CAVOUR class, 11 cruisers, and 13 destroyers. The VITTORIO VENETO was struck many times by torpedoes. The cruisers POLA, ZARA, and FIUME were sunk and the destroyers VINCENZO GIOBERTI

and the MAESTRALE were also sunk. A cruiser
and a destroyer were badly damaged. The C-in-C

The Vittorio Veneto

was Admiral
Sir A. B.
Cunningham
The battle

Two of the Italian warships sunk in the Mediterranean
battle. Above, the cruiser Zara, and, below, the large
destroyer Vincenzo Gioberti.

ADMIRAL SIR A. B. CUNNINGHAM

is to be called the Battle of Cape Matapan. Italian, German, and Danish ships in American ports were siezed, to prevent acts of sabotage. British troops in Eritrea are nearing Asmara. Our forces in Abyssinia occupied Diredawa. The R.A.F. heavily raided Brest, where the SCHARNHORST and GNEISENAU

The Scharnhorst

are sheltering. Strong Army and R.A.F. reinforcements arrived in Singapore. Mr. Matsuoka, Japanese Foreign Minister arrived in Rome from Berlin. Asmara, capital of Eritrea, surrendered to British forces without any resistance by the Italians. Shipping losses for week ending March 23-24 were 59,141 tons. An Italian U-boat.

and the tanker LAURA CORRADO were sunk by one of our submarines, and an Italian destroyer fleeing from Massawa was sunk by the R.A.F. Our forces in Eritrea are rapidly approaching Massawa. The R.A.F are now using more powerful bombs. The frontier between Germany and Yugoslavia is being closed. The U.S.A. has rejected protests by Germany and Italy against the seizure of their vessels in American ports.

## The Eighty-first Week — April 3rd 1941

The German legation in Belgrade received orders from Berlin to leave at once. The Yugoslav Government declared Belgrade an open city. Count Teleki, Hungarian Prime Minister, committed suicide. M. de Bardossy became Premier in succession to Count Teleki. Rapid British advances in Abyssinia fore-shadow the early fall of Addis Ababa. Three Italian destroyers fleeing from Massawa, were sunk by naval aircraft. German mechanized forces have occupied Benghazi. Our troops had been previously withdrawn. Germany is preparing for a move against Yugoslavia. South African troops crossed the Awash River, less than 90 miles from Addis Ababa. The crews of the last Italian destroyers left in Massawa — the PANTERA and the TIGRE scuttled their ships.

Two German bombers were shot down during night raids on the West Country. Mr. Matsuoka, left Berlin for Moscow on his return to Tokio. The advance of German mechanized forces Eastwards from Benghazi was checked by our troops. Tripoly was again heavily bombed. British forces advancing southwards from Asmara took

Adowa. Reports from Irak indicate that Rashid
Ali, Nationalist Leader, is attempting to seize
power. Men in the 41, 42, and 43 age classes
registered for war work.

## GERMANY AND ITALY INVADED YUGOSLAVIA
### AND GREECE at 5.30 a.m. on April 6th 194

Belgrade was heavily bombed by the Germans.
The British Government announced that
an army had been sent to Greece, and that
the R.A.F. had been strongly reinforced. The R.A.F.
bombed motor transport in Sofia. Yugoslavia
has signed a non-aggression pact with Russia.
South African troops occupied Addis Ababa. To reach
the capital, they covered 700 miles in 28 days.
Three enemy aircraft were shot down during
night raids on this country. During the week
on all fronts the enemy lost 67 planes to
our loss of 19. Sir Kingsley Wood, Chancellor of

the Exchequer, introduced his Budget. The main
feature was the increase of income tax to 10/- in the
pound. German troops occupied Western Thrace,
in Greece. Our government broke off relations with
Hungary. Debra Marcos
was occupied by
Abyssinian Patriot forces.
Mr. Matsuoka reached
Moscow. ~~Five~~ enemy
aircraft were shot
down during night
raids on this country.

Our heaviest raid of the war was launched on
Kiel by the R.A.F. The Germans continue
to advance in Southern Yugoslavia. Merchant
shipping losses for week-ending March 30-31 were
13 British ships, 5 allied, and 2 neutral. Civilians
killed in air raids during March, numbered, 4,269,
and 5,577 were seriously injured. Seven German
bombers were shot down during night raids on

this country. German and Italian mechanized units reached Derna. Kiel was again heavily bombed by the R.A.F. Big changes in the lists of reserved occupation were announced. German troops occupied Skoplie, the capital of Serbia, and other German forces captured Salonika after fierce fighting. The Yugoslav forces on the North Albanian front captured captured Scutari. Two enemy supply ships were sunk in the Central Mediterranean. The R.A.F. launched a heavy raid on Berlin.

## The Eighty - second Week.                    April 10th 1941

Lieut.-General Sir Richard O'Connor, O.C, Western Desert, and Lieut-General Philip Neame V.C. have been captured in Libya. Lieut.-General Sir Maitland Wilson assumed command of the British troops in Greece. Hungarian forces entered Yugoslav territory. German forces advancing into Northern Greece came into contact with British

and Imperial troops. The R.A.F. continuously attacked
German columns advancing into Greece. President
Roosevelt declared that the Red Sea were no
longer within the combat zone. British and
German forces were in action at two points
in Greece - the Monastir Gap, and South and
South - West of Salonika. The Yugoslavs are
forced to give more ground. During the first
12 days of April, R.A.F. fighters and A.A. Guns
accounted for 46 night raiders over this country.
In Libya a small German mechanized column
occupied Bardia, having by-passed Tobruk. British
and Greek troops beat back the
Germans in local attacks. Free Norwegian
forces raided a port in Northern Norway,
and destroyed oil depots and harbour
works. Russia and Japan signed a pact
of friendship. Mr. Churchill broadcast a
message to the Yugoslav people. British and
Greek forces withdrew to new positions

101

in the Balkans. The R.A.F. heavily attacked Brest. Enemy infantry supported by tanks attacked Tobruk but were repulsed. The Duke of Aosta, Italian C-in-C in Abyssinia, requested a safe conduct for an envoy to General Cunningham's headquarters at Diredawa. The British cruiser BONAVENTURA (5,450 tons) was sunk while acting as escort vessel. The British submarine TIGRIS has sunk an enemy tanker bound for France. The night raids on Britain were chiefly

H.M.S. Bonaventure

in Northern Ireland. Eight of the raiders were shot down. An entire enemy convoy of 3 Italian destroyers, 5 supply ships bound for Libya were wiped out by British naval forces. Allied troops in Greece are engaged in a big battle in Western Macedonia.

Organised resistance to the Germans in Yugoslavia is over. London had one of its severest night raids of the war. During this raid Lord Stamp, his wife and son were killed. Five Nazi bombers were shot down. British bombers raided Heligoland and France by day and Brest and Bremen by night.

LORD STAMP

## The Eighty-third Week                    April 17th. 1941.

Anglo-Greek forces are engaged in a fierce battle with the Germans, near Mt. Olympus. In Libya an attack on Tobruk was repulsed with heavy losses to the enemy. Berlin endured its heaviest raid. Our new Short-Stirling bombers were used. Portsmouth was the chief target of the enemy night raiders. 3 were shot down. Violent fighting continued all along the Greek front. Britain announced that if Cairo or Athens are bombed, Rome will be also bombed. Alexander Korizis, Greek Prime Minister, died. Strong Imperial forces arrived in Irak to open up lines of communication. Fierce fighting continued in Greece. King George of Greece formed a military cabinet, with himself as Premier. There was a fairly heavy raid on London. About 300,000 women of the 1920 class registered for national service. Our main forces in Greece have withdrawn to a shorter line. Another German attack on Tobruk was repulsed. A second German U-boat ace, Captain Schepke was sunk with his U-boat in the Atlantic. Our naval forces heavily bombarded Tripoli. German night raiders concentrated against Plymouth. 3 enemy supply ships were sunk in the Mediterranean. Our forces in Greece took up new positions South of Lamia.

In Abyssinia our troops began to attack Dessie. Plymouth was again the chief objective of the enemy night raiders. Our night bombers launched a heavy attack on Brest. The Greek armies of the Epirus and Macedonia capitulated to the Germans. The loss of the armed merchant cruiser RAJPUTANA (16,644 tons) was announced by the Admiralty. Plymouth was heavily attacked by Nazi raiders. Brest was again fiercely attacked by the R.A.F.

The armed merchant cruiser H.M.S. Rajputana, which has been sunk by torpedo action.

The Eighty-fourth Week                April 24th 1941

Kiel shipyards were heavily attacked by our bombers. Portsmouth was the chief objective-of the enemy night bombers. The Italians were routed in a fierce battle near Dessie. The British submarine URGE, torpedoed and sank an enemy oil tanker. The U.S. Navy is to patrol and protect the Western Atlantic. Our advance on Dessie continues. Viscount Gort, V.C. was appointed Governor and C.-in-C. of Gibraltar. Allied forces in Greece continued to fall back, but making the Germans pay dearly. Another attack on Tobruk was repulsed. In Greece, our rearguards continued to fight gallantly to cover the withdrawal of our main forces. Hamburg was heavily attacked by our night bombers. German forces entered Athens. Light enemy columns crossed the frontier into Egypt. During the week-ending April

26, the enemy lost 80 planes. Our losses were 35. Our main forces began their withdrawal from Greece. After a hard fight at Combolchia Pass, South African troops entered Dessie. Emden was heavily attacked during daylight. It Out of the original Empire force of 60,000 men in Greece, 48,000 have so far been successfully withdrawn. Plymouth was again raided by the Germans. 12,000 Nazi troops, with tanks and artillery have arrived in Finland. Up to the end of March air-raid casualties in Britain numbered 69,000 - nearly 29,000 killed and 40,000 injured.

---

The Eighty - fifth Week        May 1st 1941
        Lord Beaverbrook became Minister of State while his successor as Minister of Aircraft Production was Lt.-Col. J.T.C. Moore-Brabazon, former Minister of Transport. The ministries of

Transport and shipping were merged with Mr.
Leathers as Minister. More Iraki troops were
concentrated near Habbaniyah Aerodrome.
Another attack on Tobruk was repulsed. The U.S. have
arranged to place 50 tankers at our disposal.
Iraki troops shelled the British
cantonment at Habbaniyah. The Pro-
Axis Iraki Premier, Rashid Ali, was
appealing to Hitler for military aid.
Merseyside was the main target of
enemy night raiders. British troops seized the docks
and airport at Basra. Fighting continued at Habbaniyah.
Merseyside was again attacked by enemy night raiders.
16 German bombers were destroyed. Our heaviest night
attack was on Cologne. Women aged 21 registered
for war service. Mr. Churchill broadcast a message
of hope to Poland. Our troops at Habbaniyah were
reinforced from Basra. Our forces continue to
make progress in Abyssinia. The R.A.F. again
bombed the SCHARNHORST and GNEISENAU at Brest.

Clydeside, Merseyside, and Northern Ireland bore the brunt of night raids on this country. 9 enemy planes were shot down. We launched a heavy raid on Mannheim. Major-General Freyburg. V.C. was appointed c-in-c of the allied forces in Crete. A two days debate on the conduct of the war started in the House of Commons. Stalin took over the Premiership of Soviet Russia. R.A.F. bombed Iraki transport and guns. Axis troops seized the islands of Mitylene and Chios, off the coast of Turkey. 9 enemy fighters were destroyed by our in raids over this country. Clydeside was the main target. Iraki troops in the Habbaniyah area were dispersed after losing 1,000 men. Merseyside, Humber district and the Bristol Channel area were all sharply raided. 24 enemy planes were shot down. Brest was again raided by the R.AF.

During the day 15 enemy planes were shot down and 14 during the night. 300 of our bombers raided Hamburg and Bremen. Mr. Bevin announced the formation of a reserve pool of officers and men for the Merchant Navy. The casualties of the A.I.F. in Greece number 3,000. Our shipping loses for April were:- 60 British ships, 43 allied ships, and 3 neutral. The British cruiser CORNWALL has sunk an enemy raider in the Indian Ocean. London was again heavily raided, and the House of Commons, Westminster Abbey,

The damaged altar of Westminster Abbey, which was bombed during the week-end.

RUDOLF HESS

the British Museum, and other famous buildings were damaged. Admiralty figures put Axis shipping losses during the past six weeks at over 600,000 tons. Lt.-General Sir Maitland Wilson was appointed G.O.C. of the British forces in Palestine and Transjordan. The German supply ship COBURG, was intercepted by the Australian cruiser CANBERRA and the New Zealand cruiser LEANDER in the Indian Ocean. 9 German bombers were brought down during night raids on this country. Rudolf Hess, Hitler's Deputy, landed in Scotland, on the night of Saturday, May 10th. Benghazi was bombarded by the Navy. Mannheim was severely raided by R.A.F.

The Eighty-seventh Week.    May 15th 1941

British bombers bombed German planes on Syrian airfields. Strong re-inforcements arrived in Singapore. Out of the 437,000 British

111

troops sent to France during the Continental fighting. 384,000. including wounded, were brought away, 40,000 were captured, and 13,000 killed. Of 23,800 British troops sent to Norway, 22,600 were brought away. 250 killed, and 950 captured. Well-known buildings damaged in recent raids on London included St. James's Palace, Queen's Hall, the London Museum, St. Clement Danes Church, and Lambeth Palace. American coastguards boarded the NORMANDIE and 10 French ships and took them into "protective custody". The Italian forces in Amba Alagi were surrounded by our forces. The Duke of Aosta, Viceroy of Abyssinia and Italian C-in-C, sent an emissary to General Cunningham to seek terms of surrender. Men in the age 39 class registered for service. An intensive attack on the French Channel ports was made by our bombers. 21 German aircraft were destroyed and others damaged in the Middle East.

<u>The Eighty-seventh Week (continued)</u>   <u>May 18th 1941</u>

American Federal Agents began a nation-wide round-up of aliens. The Duke of Spoleto, brother of the Duke of Aosta, was proclaimed King of Croatia, formerly part of Yugoslavia. R.A.F. bombers attacked Kiel and Emden. The 8,299-ton liner ZAMZAM was sunk by a Nazi raider in the South Atlantic. Vice-Admiral J. Whitworth was appointed Second Sea Lord and Chief of Naval Personnel. The Germans have attempted to storm Crete with paratroops and air-borne forces wearing New-Zealand battle-dress. Fallujah, 35 miles from Bagdad was captured by our forces in Iraq. The House of Commons passed the Fire Services Bill.

The Zamzam

Fierce fighting continued in Crete especially around Maleme and Suda Bay. The Duke of Aosta and five Italian Generals formally surrendered to representatives of General Cunningham. German concentrations in by Libya were heavily attacked by the R.A.F. In Iraq we captured a post 25 miles from Rutba. Berlin requested America to withdraw all her diplomatic staff from Paris by June 10th.

THE DUKE OF AOSTA

## The Eighty-eighth Week                    May 22nd 1941

The fighting in Crete continued with still greater intensity. Our submarines have sunk a troopship and a tanker bound for Libya. German paratroops are being landed in great numbers in Crete. In a battle off Greenland H.M.S. HOOD was blown up by an unlucky hit in the magazine from the BISMARCK.

H.M.S. Hood, sunk in the naval battle off the coast of Greenland.

Two of the principal German troop-carrying planes. Top, the Focke-Wulf Condor, which has accommodation for about thirty troops. Bottom, the Junkers 89, which can take about forty men.

The position in Crete is still critical. An attempt on life of King Victor Emmanuel was made by a Greek. All the shots missed. The Germans heavily bombed Canea, Retimo and Candia in Crete. One torpedo hit by our naval aircraft was obtained on the BISMARCK. King George of Greece has left Crete for Cairo. The Germans have lost 250 aircraft in Crete. The Germans have penetrated our defences West of Canea. The frontiers of Syria were closed by the French authorities. The Admiralty issued a full account of the sinking of the BISMARCK. The Admiralty also announced

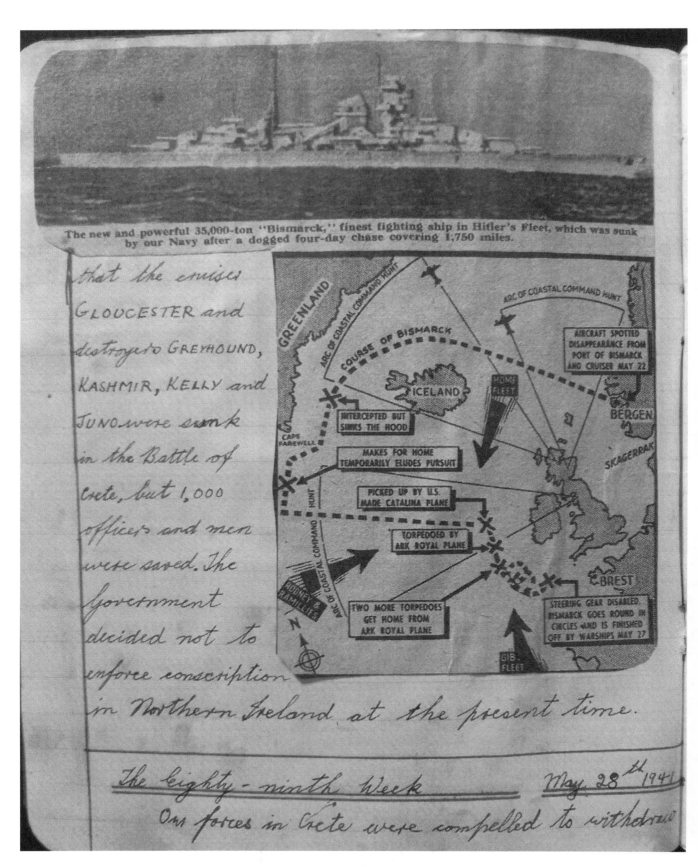

The new and powerful 35,000-ton "Bismarck," finest fighting ship in Hitler's Fleet, which was sunk by our Navy after a dogged four-day chase covering 1,750 miles.

that the cruiser GLOUCESTER and destroyer GREYHOUND, KASHMIR, KELLY and JUNO were sunk in the Battle of Crete, but 1,000 officers and men were saved. The Government decided not to enforce conscription in Northern Ireland at the present time.

<u>The Eighty-ninth Week</u>                    <u>May. 28<sup>th</sup> 1941</u>

Our forces in Crete were compelled to withdraw

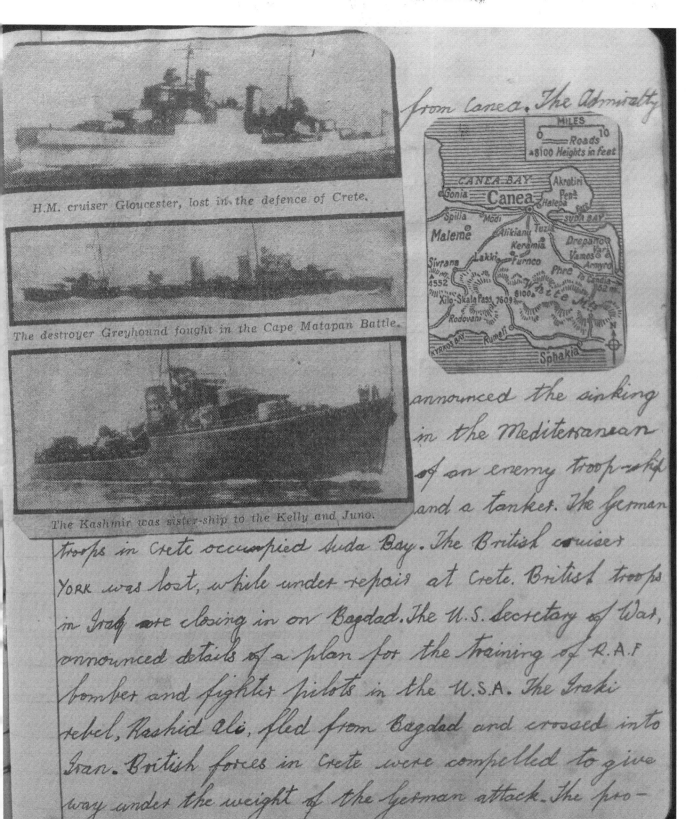

H.M. cruiser Gloucester, lost in the defence of Crete.

The destroyer Greyhound fought in the Cape Matapan Battle.

The Kashmir was sister-ship to the Kelly and Juno.

from Canea. The Admiralty announced the sinking in the Mediterranean of an enemy troop-ship and a tanker. The German troops in Crete occupied Suda Bay. The British cruiser YORK was lost, while under repair at Crete. British troops in Iraq are closing in on Bagdad. The U.S. Secretary of War, announced details of a plan for the training of R.A.F bomber and fighter pilots in the U.S.A. The Iraki rebel, Rashid Ali, fled from Bagdad and crossed into Iran. British forces in Crete were compelled to give way under the weight of the German attack. The pro-

Nazi revolt in Iraq has collapsed. The Imperial forces were withdrawn from Crete. The Admiralty announced the loss of the armed merchant cruiser SALOPIAN (10,540). Air Vice-Marshal Arthur Tedder was appointed Air Officer C-in-C Middle East. The rationing of clothing in this country was announced. Hitler and Mussolini met at the Brenner Pass. General Weygand flew from Syria to Vichy to confer with M. Petain. France said that she has decided to defend Syria and Tunisia single-handed against any possible British attack. A new Iraki Cabinet was formed under the Premiership of Jamil Madfai. Two enemy supply-ships were sunk off the Tunisian coast by the R.A.F.

## The Nineteenth Week                    June 4th 1941

The Midlands were the main target for the enemy night raiders of which five were destroyed. Youths of 17, may now volunteer for the R.N and F.A.A. Wilhelm II, ex-Kaiser of Germany, died at Doorn, in Holland. There were further reports of large-scale Nazi infiltration into Syria. Three enemy supply-ships and a trawler were sunk, following the operations against the BISMARCK, by the Royal Navy. Sir Stafford Cripps, our Ambassador to Moscow, ~~was~~ is on his way to London to confer with the Foreign Secretary. Our forces in Abyssinia, attacked Jimma and took 1,000 Italian prisoners. Alexandria was heavily raided by the Germans.

## ALLIED FORCES ENTERED SYRIA ON JUNE 8th

Another 4,000 Italians were captured in Abyssinia. The French islands of Martinique and Guadeloupe are to be patrolled by U.S. warships and planes. Our forces advanced 40 miles into Syria after encountering slight resistance. The Admiralty announced that during the evacuation from Crete the following additional ships have been lost: the anti-aircraft cruiser CALCUTTA

## Stockings On The Stocks

A WOMAN correspondent writes: Make a note of No. 787. This will stand for a new, finer version of the 1943 best-selling utility stockings, No. 731. The Board of Trade have this week issued directions to manufacturers to produce the new stockings, which will come at about 2s 9d a pair. It will be some months before they reach the shops. There is little likelihood of additional fully-fashioned stockings made this year. Some fully-fashioned sub-standard service stockings which were to be dyed black and issued to the public are no longer available. The Ministry of Supply have made other arrangements for their disposal.

_To be continued
in
Volume II_

Printed by Amazon Italia Logistica S.r.l.
Torrazza Piemonte (TO), Italy